WALKING THROUGH THE WOODS

by

Sister Mary Francilene Van de Vyver, CSSF

D0757003

Jeremiah Press
Boca Raton, Florida

Cover Photo: Kensington Metropark
Milford, Michigan

Taken by Dr. Dan Benvenisti, M.D., F.A.C.P.
Hematology and Oncology
St. Mary Hospital
Livonia, Michigan

Editing: Laurence Rudnicki
Camera-ready processing: Helen Copado

Copies of book available from:
Madonna University Bookstore
36600 Schoolcraft
Livonia, Michigan 48150
(313) 591-5088

All proceeds from this book go toward the support of the
Madonna University Scholarship Endowment.

ISBN: 1-883520-05-3
Library of Congress Catalog Card Number: 94-078049

Published by:
Jeremiah Press, Inc.
Boca Raton, Florida

Printed and bound in the United States of America

DEDICATIONS

I ask the reader to accept this work as a personal reflection of my encounters with God, myself and all those who gift my life. Without a doubt, each of us during our lifetime, will experience new waves of fear, pain, loss, hope and joy. Mine came as a result of having cancer.

I dedicate this book to my parents, family, friends and the Felician Sisters--each person who contributes to the joy of my life. Above all, I dedicate this work as I have done so with my life--in response to the Lord who is the source of my being.

ACKNOWLEDGEMENTS

I extend gratitude to the caring people who work with great dedication at:

Madonna University, Livonia, Michigan
St. Mary Hospital, Livonia, Michigan
Harper Hospital, Detroit, Michigan

Dilegua, o notte!
Tramontate, stelle!
Tramontate, stelle!
All'alba vincero!
VINCERO!
VINCERO!

"Nessun Dorma"
from *Turandot*
by Giacomo Puccini

ABOUT THE AUTHOR
Sister Mary Francilene Van de Vyver, CSSF

"Sister, you have cancer!" These four words from her doctor in 1992 dramatically changed the world of a vibrant, successful, and faithful Felician Sister.

Sister Mary Francilene, the eldest of six children of Hector and Irene Van de Vyver, was born in Detroit, Michigan in 1941. She graduated from the Felician Academy in 1959 and entered the religious congregation of the Felician Sisters, pronouncing final vows in 1967. During the course of her training, Sister Francilene received a Bachelor of Arts degree in music from Madonna College and a Master's in Music Education and a Doctorate in Higher Education Administration from Wayne State University.

In 1976, Sister Francilene was appointed the fifth president of Madonna College (renamed University in 1991.) Recognition and awards bestowed upon her for her accomplishments are numerous, including being named one of the "100 Most Effective College Presidents in the United States."

This reflective work is a poignant autobiographical account of a two-year portion of one life with its new combination of pain, struggle and joy.

Above all, it is a celebration of encounters — with God, with oneself and with others who lovingly share life's journey through the peaks and valleys.

CHAPTER ONE

TURNING FIFTY AND SURVIVING

September 6, 1991 turned out to be one of the most exciting days of my life. I had awakened early so as to enjoy every moment of "turning fifty." Many of my friends had joked about graveyard decorations--none of which emerged, for which I was grateful. Instead, my office staff, friends and family planned a surprise-filled experience. I began receiving a telephone call every five or ten minutes. Little did I suspect that my youngest sister had given everyone a quota of calls to make so that I would receive a minimum of fifty before the end of the day. How was she to know that my secretary was not able to be in for the day and the remainder of the staff kept forwarding the calls, which I'm sure for them were nothing but interruptions!

I was expecting a call from Greece where our Belgian cousins, Freddy and Gerda Vercammen, were spending a holiday. The week before, Gerda had placed a call to me that she and her husband would be visiting Greece over my birthday weekend and would make sure they would call the morning of September 6th. These two relatives were

WALKING THROUGH THE WOODS

special people in the lives of my family and me. Having
been born in Antwerp, Belgium in 1909, our dad had come
with his parents and brother to America in 1916, but
through the years had kept in contact with family members.
I knew Freddy and Gerda from having visited Belgium and
they had traversed the Atlantic many times for family
visits.

Little did I know that Freddy and Gerda had actually
planned to surprise me with a visit on my fiftieth birthday,
so that when the call came from "Greece," the placement
of the phone call was actually from the local Holiday Inn
and within five minutes of the call both of these cousins
were in my office without anyone knowing their
whereabouts! Needless to say, I was speechless.

The entire weekend was a truly joyful experience with
gifts, wishes, a family reunion over a "birthday brunch"--
and lots of love and affirmation.

How unaware was I that a few weeks later and well
throughout the entire next year, I would experience
anxiety, pain, surgery, treatments and examinations, and
would know the emotions of fear, love, joy, depression and
hope in new combinations.

As I recall now, I had actually experienced discomfort
due to diarrhea, constant mucous eliminations and,
eventually, some blood during bowel movements, for a
number of months before I acknowledged this condition to
anyone. Actually, as might be typical of a person who has
access to a well stocked library, I spent a few hours
reviewing the medical books of Madonna University on the
topic of gastro-intestinal problems and self diagnosed

mucous colitus as the problem, which I ascertained would be corrected with a simple addition of high fibre foods to my diet.

Fortunately, in August of 1991, when I visited Dr. Mitchell ("Dr. Mike") Rasak, a doctor friend, for a vitamin B-12 injection, he responded gently yet firmly that these symptoms ought not remain unchecked. What followed was a series of examinations by gastroenterologist, Dr. Ramon Joseph. To me he was outstanding because I had entered the examination room with tremendous fear and trepidation, all of which he countered with understanding; describing each movement as the examination proceeded. I respected this method of involving the patient in his ongoing dictation of the visit as well as the thorough description of the possible outcomes.

The results indicated the presence of a large mass, later determined to be a polyp with the medical name of "villous adenoma." Due to the size and placement of the mass, two successive operations were scheduled in October and December of 1991. Outside of experiencing a discomfort while sitting, nothing else seemed unusual and I felt my health improve as I went about my regular work as president of Madonna University, Livonia, Michigan.

This University has been and continues to be a wonderful community in which to live and work. I had begun the sixteenth year serving as its president and often recalled the fascinating words of the Chinese philosopher, Lao Tzu, "To lead the people, walk behind them." It was an exciting journey in administration to observe, inspire and interact with a dynamic and dedicated group of administrators, faculty and staff, who, together with an ever burgeoning student body of more than 4,400, constitute the largest Catholic Franciscan University in the United States.

But I haven't always been a university president. Turning fifty gave me the perfect opportunity to look back over my own personal history and marvel how God had sustained me throughout all the years and what a tremendous gift the people in my life have been.

The late William Saroyan, a prolific American storyteller, has often said, "People is all there is, all there ever was, and all there ever will be." I believe him. Could that one book describe all the relationships and people interwoven in and through the fabric of one's life, but this is not possible. In writing about my family, friends and colleagues I trust that others not mentioned by name realize that they, too, are just as gratefully remembered in my prayers and thoughts.

I was born on September 6, 1941. As the eldest child of Hector and Irene Van de Vyver, I prefaced a total of six children, all born within six and one half years. We were never in want for companionship and we often paired off: Patricia (that was my name) and Joanne, Margaret and Joyce and then the two youngest, Ronald and Gerard. Our memories are very vivid, and since we were born so close to each other, there is a "common fund" from which to draw remembrances. I name only a few, such as the annual photo our mother enclosed in the Christmas mail in which we invariably sat or stood all in a line, the eldest to the youngest, with the girls in similar dresses sewed by mother and the boys in bow tie and slicked back hair. There was one year the picture differed. It was taken in the house off the lake by "Busia" (grandmother) and "Dziadzia" (grandfather), the parents of our mother. That time we sat on the top of a large bureau and each of the girls wore her own style of skirt, blouse or dress, but most often we dressed alike. I never really minded until I got older and wanted to dress differently and wear nylons which my youngest sister would not yet be allowed.

Our favorite memory is that of the frequent Sunday afternoons we spent as a family out at Belle Isle, a large city-owned island of Detroit, Michigan, the city in which we were born and raised. Often we would all squeeze into the family car and visit the Children's Zoo and the Botanical Gardens. The highlight of the afternoon, however, was driving across the Ambassador Bridge to Canada. We would sit quietly in the car as the officer at the customs booth would inquire as to the country of our origin. Our father always hoped the officer would ask where he was born because he enjoyed pulling out his citizenship papers and telling the story of how he and his family came from Belgium. Now as I recall, I don't think the customs people really cared. But we always knew our father was disappointed when he didn't have the chance to pull out his papers because the officer hurriedly sent us on our way!

We would spend one or two hours at the water's edge in one of the parks of Windsor, Ontario, eating ice cream and watching all the people sitting in the gardens or just walking past. Many times the people would smile at the six of us enjoying our ice cream. We were very well behaved children. Part of it was probably due to living during the hard times of World War II and learning how to stand in lines for food as our mother took all six of us when she received the monthly allotment of food stamps. The two youngest baby boys would be in the "buggy" and the four of us girls holding on--two on each side.

But we sure liked our Sunday afternoons. For fun, I remember a few times when we would pretend that we lived in Canada and we'd begin shouting, "Papa ve vant to go to Amerika!" Then we would laugh as father shooed us into the car for the return trip home to Detroit.

As I write these thoughts, I am so grateful that our parents are living close to us. My sisters and brothers who are married have brought tremendous joy to our parents with the total of sixteen grandchildren and two "greats." As of this writing, our dad is in his eighties and mother in her seventies. Their hair is white and there have been many physical changes as observed in the photos taken through the years, but ours is a legacy of a loving family-- of parents who have sacrificed savings for themselves so their children could attend parochial grade schools and high schools; who have instilled a set of values for living and sharing that have molded us into a family which treasures each Christmas gathering more than the past one; and parents whose only riches are counted by the talents, hearts, minds and souls of their children and grandchildren.

As for me, I most often ask the Lord in prayer, "How can you be so good to me? I want for nothing...." From my earliest childhood desires stood forth that one constant prayer--to be a nun. There was never anything else I wanted to be, so it was not surprising that just before my fourteenth birthday I entered the Felician Academy as an "aspirant" of the Felician Sisters--a Franciscan community of Catholic nuns, originally founded (1855) in Poland by Blessed Mary Angela Truszkowska.

In looking back on the years in religious life (1992 marking the thirty-third anniversary since my entrance as a postulant, the first level of study for the sisterhood), I do not know where all of these years went by with such vibrancy of speed and intensity. Having studied music, I had been assigned as a music teacher for the first twelve years of ministry. I recall the classes and students I taught and the musicals directed, especially my favorite, performed at Ladywood High School--"The Sound of Music."

And now, since 1974, my life has been involved with the people of Madonna University (formerly "College" until 1991). In accepting the presidency in 1976, I did so with deep gratitude to the Felician community for entrusting this ministry to me, and with the desire to be as effective and committed as the previous four presidents: Sisters Mary Paula, Assumpta, Raynelda and Danatha--all of whom I had known except the first, and especially the fourth,Sister Mary Danatha, who was a most perceptive mentor and model.

By 1992 my life was in a well balanced mode of work, prayer, study, and relaxation. I had arrived at the prime of life with few problems but with many opportunities to be creative, involved, and above all, peacefully settled in a life

7

that I enjoyed and that was meaningful in its commitment. Did I realize that everything I had ever read or heard or experienced prior to my fiftieth year was in preparation for the next part of my life's journey?

CHAPTER TWO

NOTHING IS EVER ROUTINE

On January 6, 1992, I was scheduled for what I thought would be a routine follow-up visit with Dr. Robert Lilly, general surgeon at St. Mary Hospital, Livonia, Michigan. After a second surgery in December 1991 for the removal of a rectal polyp, I was feeling great and expected that the visit would be a discussion of diet and perhaps some suggestions for avoiding continued irritation of the bowel.

It was the end of a busy work day in my office at Madonna University and as I entered the doctor's examination room I recall that my thoughts were very upbeat and I expected nothing out of the ordinary. In fact, I had not even disrobed, thinking that the appointment would be a fast one just to review the test results. We both sat next to each other in the two chairs available in one of the examination rooms.

"Well, how do you feel?" questioned Dr. Lilly in his baritone voice. "Just great, Doctor," I said, optimistically. Next came one of the most unusual experiences of my life. What I heard from the doctor seemed to be spoken about someone else, but not me.

"I wish I could tell you everything is fine and that I had good news," Dr. Lilly said, "but the pathology reports on the last polyp removal indicates that you have colorectal cancer."

I felt as if I were hearing this diagnosis about another person. It was the most detached feeling I've ever had. After a moment, I asked Dr. Lilly to "run that by me again." He did exactly that, in a calm, reassuring way, but my mind was racing. How could this be possible? I was feeling so much better than two months previous to this and I never gave a thought to having anything more than polyps. "Why would the report indicate cancer now when the first polyp removal did not indicate any such malignancy?" I questioned him, thinking there must be some mistake.

Dr. Lilly was thorough in his explanations, as I wanted him to be. The pathology report following the December surgery had indicated negative on the polyp tissue but malignancy in the bowel wall itself. Dr. Lilly proceeded to pull out his colored diagrams and charts portraying the digestive system. At that moment I had a sudden flashback to college Biology 101 with Sister Mary Danatha as she described to us in great detail the functions of the stomach, small intestine, colon and rectum. I then felt even more removed from the moment. This discussion was about "a" human body -- not mine!

Reality began to set in as Dr. Lilly described the type of operation which should be performed as soon as possible to minimize any growth in the tumor. The tumor would have to be removed as well as a portion of the large bowel (approximately six or seven inches above the rectum) surrounding the tumor. I still had hope.

"Unfortunately, Sister, we won't be able to save the rectum nor the sphincter muscle, as you see here on the diagram, because the tumor is too low in the rectum," indicated the surgeon with all the years of experience he had knowing all too well the full extent of the procedure before I would realize the impact of this news.

"Does this mean a colostomy?" I inquired as if I were asking this about a friend of mine.

"Yes," responded Dr. Lilly. I could feel his empathy for me in the kindness of his eyes and I respected him for answering me directly since I wanted to know everything about the procedure.

He then described how the anus would be closed during a colostomy surgery and the remaining section of the large bowel would be connected to a new opening in the abdomen, referred to as a "stoma."

At this point I began to realize that this was me. I felt tears in my eyes because the operation seemed such a drastic step but I experienced my mind responding, "Lord, help me to handle this."

After all my questions were answered I found a humorous moment which I laughed about with my friends many times in the following weeks. When Dr. Lilly finished his thorough explanations I countered with a challenge.

"Dr. Lilly, in these days of modern science when so many parts of the human anatomy can be successfully

11

transplanted, such as the heart, liver, and lungs, why hasn't the medical profession perfected the transplant of an ass?!"

When the visit was over I thanked the doctor and walked out of his office. Some of my friends have suggested that I should have taken a family member or friend with me into the doctor's office when he delivered the news. I don't agree with them because during the time of the actual visit, as I think back on it, the encounter was a very personal one. Two human beings were discussing a life situation which both knew would generate a strong level of trust in the days ahead.

The full impact of our discussion, however, hit me once I left the office and entered the elevator. In fact, I found myself thinking, "Can anyone see that I have cancer?" I remember being overwhelmed with the feeling that I had to tell somebody the news I had just received. I immediately planned to locate my youngest sister, Sister Joyce Marie, a member of our Felician Order who worked at St. Mary Hospital as the Director of its Child Care Center. I walked hurriedly to the elevator.

Another woman from a neighboring office entered the elevator with me. I had noticed her locking a door as I passed along the corridor. We acknowledged each other with small talk. "Did you have a nice New Year?" "Yes, thank you." Then I blurted out, "Actually, I just left my doctor's office and he told me I have cancer!" I suppose I shocked her with my sudden outburst, but I felt at that overwhelming moment I couldn't wait another minute before telling someone, anyone, what I had just heard.

When the elevator opened on the first floor, any

passer-by observing the scene witnessed two women spontaneously hugging each other. As we walked out into the street level she offered encouraging words, "So many advances are being made everyday with various treatments, I'm sure you'll be just fine."

I treasure the memory of that moment. The woman did not know me but she offered a beautiful expression of caring. In all the days and months ahead, my family and friends would be my strongest supports, but at the minutes of first knowledge, I experienced a simple spontaneous affirmation, a moment not based upon any prior knowledge or commitment, a touch of gratuitous kindness.

The Van de Vyver family on a Sunday outing to the Belle Isle Botanical Gardens, Circa 1951.

CHAPTER THREE

FACING THE FACULTY

I couldn't sleep much during the night and early morning hours just before Friday, January 10, 1992. Our monthly meeting for the faculty members of Madonna University was scheduled for that day. A few had heard by way of the "rumor mill" that I might be gone for an extended medical leave. I didn't want to "drop out" that way. Here was a group of cherished people, many of whom I had worked with in the "Lord's vineyard" at Madonna University for the past eighteen years, sixteen as its president.

Some faculty members had undergone cancer surgery and other serious illnesses throughout the years. We knew each other. Here was my "extended family" and I was anxious as to what I could say that would allow them and me to share an extremely vulnerable and human moment. The topic for my actual presentation on the agenda was a discussion regarding the budget and fiscal challenges facing the University. It was time for the"pulling-in-the-belt" homily! The faculty were receptive and after the presentation I plunged ahead into a most personal

15

reflection.

I told them about my experience at the doctor's office and that I would be undergoing surgery the following week. I asked for their prayers and told them how much my involvement with each member meant to me.

To close my announcement, I shared an inspirational message that I had copied down on a small card some thirty-five years ago after reading the inspiring work, *The Night They Burned The Mountain,* by Dr.Thomas Dooley. This account of his confrontation with cancer had made a strong impact on me during my youth. I had copied down one of the passages, thinking that sometime in my life perhaps I would like to share this with others. Indeed, I have referred to it on many occasions, never thinking I would be in need of this very message.

...My dream. The mountain in my dream was burned, and now, new life was being planted into near dead soil. I must plant new seedlings of life into the burnt soil of my personal mountain of sadness. I must cultivate new fields of food to feed those who cannot feed themselves.

No more self-sadness, no darkness, no anger at God for my cancer. There was no cancer in my spirit. The Lord saw to it. I would keep my appetite for fruitful activity.

In the midst of winter I suddenly found there was in me an invincible summer. I could now be tender in a better way--I shared in the fellowship of pain.

16

Facing the Faculty

How much these words resounded in my own heart as I stood together with the faculty. Immediately after the meeting many colleagues came up to share words and embraces with me. Those who had undergone the pain, surgery and resurrection from cancer experiences surrounded me with hugs and loving support--Marilee, Terrie, Joy, Bess. Other faculty members--Linette, Charlotte, Sister Cecilia, Mary, Larry, and so many others evidenced an empathy I feel until this day.

After the faculty meeting, Dr. Jim Reilly, one of our dedicated "long-termers" said, "Sister Francilene, you always do such a good job at these faculty meetings, but this was the best one ever."

He knew it and I knew it. Not because of what I said, but because the personal message was one which superseded agenda items, budget matters and academic disciplines. It was a moment of human vulnerability.

Our parents, Hector and Irene Van de Vyver pictured with the statue of St. Francis of Assisi they donated to Madonna University, 1993.

CHAPTER FOUR

POETRY -- MUSINGS OF THE SOUL IN A BATTERED BODY

Death came, you know,
The other night, or so.
In darkness;
The swiftness
      of engulfing waves.
It came quite fast,
Careening past.
I know, or knew not,
Nor could want to care.

      In bolts of velours;
      Swishing, shadowing--
      Seeking to grasp
         a human form;
      Uninformed.

            Death came, you know,
            The other night, or so.
            But into its own darkness
            Did steps retrace.

                                    ("Preparation," 1964)

19

WALKING THROUGH THE WOODS

I had written this poem to Sister Mary Damascene, one of my former teachers, after she sustained a serious automobile accident.

The night before surgery as I lay in the hospital bed with plenty of time to think, the words of this poem echoed in my mind. The room was very quiet, with little movement occuring out in the corridor. I didn't feel like turning on the television. I wanted to think about my life and the impending experience I would undergo in about twelve hours. There were no telephone calls, which at first I thought unusual since so many of my friends knew that I was hospitalized that afternoon. The following morning, I came to find out that inadvertently the phone jack in the room I was in had been placed into an inactive outlet. Numerous family and friends called but couldn't get through because all they heard was a busy signal. Each one thought I was speaking to someone else, while in reality I was alone with my thoughts. (That was another well planned incident I attribute to the Lord who wanted me to Himself for a couple of hours without any interruptions.)

I wasn't afraid. All the past weeks, months and even years, I had a tremendous fear of pain, of examinations, of doctors in general. That evening, I wasn't afraid. I thought about my poem, and even though death might be at my doorstep because of the general uncertainty in any surgery--there is never a 100% guarantee about any day of life--I came to feel held in the palm of the Lord's hand as I had read in Isaiah so many times (49:15-16). I experienced a feeling of trust that claimed a new level in my soul. I cried a few tears of deep gratitude for this depth of understanding of what it meant to give everything to the Lord--my talents, my fears, my joys, my family, our Felician community, Madonna University and my position, my fifty years of life with the fabric of its memories--even to the point of saying, "Lord, I give you myself in death if that is what you want. I would like to live more years to serve and to love, BUT, if this is the moment of your second coming into my life--I can really trust you without fear."

In all the days and nights since then, so often this prayer, which I call one of "non-preference or abandonment to God," has re-echoed in my soul at other moments and it is a great grace which I attribute to God's mercy and overwhelming loving kindness to me. It was worth the cancer in my body to release the strength and joy that resided in my soul when I came to that moment of facing God in trust.

Every poet seeks avenues in which to share the poetic musings of the inner self. Perhaps it is because we want to share those experiences of the human condition which bind us one to another. Poetry, like music, swells from the deep recesses of the soul as emotional responses to experiences which cannot well be captured by speech or prosaic expressions. Often these are simply utterings of words or phrases which hope to portray a glimpse of a deeply felt moment. In this chapter, I want to share a few such poems. I believe each poem speaks for itself without unnecessary explanations.

WALKING THROUGH THE WOODS

WHO'S WHO?

Man 1 - Oh! Great and mighty is the
             human mind!

Man 2 - Why?

Man 1 - Yesterday I flew beyond the
             stars.

Man 2 - Oh?

Man 1 - Tomorrow's moon finds me
             walking upon her face.

Man 2 - But ...

Man 1 - None surpass man; his awful
             might!

Man 2 - Well, there...

Man 1 - Why, I've made ships and
             cars and light and speed.

Man 2 - Oh, but I ...

Man 1 - I've made them all; have
             scaled the highest mount.

Man 2 - No, because I...

Man 1 - You? What could you
             attempt to make?

Man 2 - I made...

Man 1 - There is not much I've left
             for you to do.

Man 2 - Perhaps not much,
             but I made you.

                           (1985)

A GOSPEL VISIT
(Matthew 7:7-10, John 6:34-38, John 4:10-15)

Knock.
Barely a rap.
Or was it even that?
Perhaps only a timid wisp
        of early morning wind
        brushing through the crevice.
No begger would ever rap so lightly
Were he starving for his daily bread.
It would be one knock, of course;
But a hungry one.

Knock.
Barely a tap.
Or was it more than that?
Perhaps only the last vestiges
        of the pre-dawn's rainfall
        spattering upon the oaken door.
No woman would ever tap so lightly
Were she in need of fresh water.
It would be one knock, of course;
But a thirsty one.

Knock.
Barely a touch.
Or was it that much?
Perhaps only a distant thud

23

WALKING THROUGH THE WOODS

from thawing snow-ladened roofs.
No lover would ever brush so lightly
Were the loved one behind the door.
It would be one knock, of course;
But an anxious one.

Knock.
And so I often stand outside the door and fret--
Hungry,
Thirsty,
Anxious;
Until once again you put trust into my timid heart
And such strength into a knocking hand.

(1973)

AND THE YEARS SPEAK

You call me ancient,
    and so I am.
You name me elderly,
    and my tongue doesn't resist the label.
You count my years,
    tho' I have let a few slip by unnoticed.

But
I wear my age
    with dignity.
I bear the years
    with pride unbent
    (not like my stooped frame).
I've learned to face joy, pain, God,
    and death
    with equal amounts of hope and fear;
    hope still being in the majority.

But
I can't yet learn to trust my own future.
Too much is held in your younger hands.

(1985)

WALKING THROUGH THE WOODS

ASH WEDNESDAY
(Luke 9:4-5)

Dust.
Oh, residue of action.
Trampled upon,
Buried beneath,
Blown over,
Wiped away
from the tables of men.

Dust.
Oh, product of humanity.
Often overlooked,
Somewhat ignored,
At times disdained,
Forever banned
from the houses of men.

Dust.
At once both the breath
And fulfillment of life.
The substance from which
God has formed a man,
And that to which man is again returned
After the spirit and life-blood
Have long been inhabitants.

Dust.
Only once were you asked to leave--
From the shoes of the town
Which did not welcome the peace and
the spirit of God.

(Printed in *The Cord,* Volume 33, No. 2
February, 1983. p. 39)

WALKING THROUGH THE WOODS

JOHN 1 : 1

In the beginning was the Word.
The Word was God.
God was Love.

Now is the Word.
The Word is God.
God loves.

Now you are.
God's Word is in you.
God loves through you.

Now, I am.
God's Word is spoken
And received.

I love.

(1973)

CHAPTER FIVE

PAIN--A FORGOTTEN COMPANION

A phenomenon of the human memory is that one forgets the physical pain that accompanies recuperation from surgery. Time has passed since my hospitalization for colon cancer surgery, the stay in the critical care unit and subsequent weeks of healing, but as I recall the emotions of the day of surgery and those first few post-operative weeks, it is often difficult to actually remember the pain.

I enjoy travelling. I used a visualization technique on the morning of surgery, January 15, 1992. Having had a restful night, a peaceful morning prayer time, and the gift of a vivid imagination, I decided to look upon this day of my life as a journey into the unknown. I usually prefer a map and a detailed agenda for each day of a trip, but this day I really "let myself go," and prayed, "Lord, you lead today. Set the course. Guide the hand of my surgeon and that of the anesthesiologist and anyone else joining me on this day's journey. Please, bring me to a safe destination. Let my body and my spirit be healed from all illness and undue anxiety. (Lord, you know how I love that part of the Mass when the celebrant prays,'protect us from all undue anxiety!'). Bless my parents, brothers and sisters and their

WALKING THROUGH THE WOODS

families, Sister Joyce, my Felician community, our University family--any person I have ever met on my life's journey to this date. Forgive me my sins, my pride, selfishness, lack of trust and charity, and above all, teach me through today's experience to follow you more closely forever. Amen."

At approximately 10:00 a.m. the "travelling coach" arrived. I had been awaiting the ET-nurse, (enterostomal therapist: a specialist in the field of stoma patients, such as I was soon to become), Carole LePage, who had promised to come and see me just before surgery to ink mark the place on my abdomen to indicate the best area to place the new opening (stoma). What to do? From my reading I recalled that a colostomy patient is advised to have a good determination made on one's body prior to surgery to make certain that the stoma would not be in a fatty crease of the stomach area, or too high or low for the appliance (elimination bag) to hang at a comfortable angle. I was sure that with my normal sized body the surgeon would have no difficulty locating the correct spot on the left side of my abdomen, but I knew I'd have a little more reassurance if Carole would appear.

Many years of being an obedient nun prompted me into action when the orderly asked that I would move from my bed onto the moveable cart. I slid over and was about to be pushed out of my room when the telephone rang. I asked the orderly to wait for a minute while I answered that last call. It was Carole! She had found the order that my surgery had been moved up by an hour and she was coming right over to see me.

30

I said to the orderly, "Can you take a coffee break, or something? My nurse is coming and I want five minutes with her, please!" No problem.

Thinking that Carole would mark my body while I was lying on the cart, I waited for her prompt arrival. Within seconds she appeared, breathless.

"Hurry," she said. "We've got to do this immediately! Let's get you off this cart."

It's great there was no candid camera hidden in the corner of that hospital room. With only seconds to spare, Carol pushed a chair over and helped me--ingloriously, with back flaps opening on my hospital gown, to slip down off the cart onto the chair so she could appropriately place the ink marks while I was seated. Meanwhile, the orderly was back from his quick coffee break and knocking on the door that he needed to move me down immediately to the OR.

Carole whispered, "Hurry, get back on the cart," as she assisted me once again to regain my prostrate position, ready for the journey to the second floor. We both smiled because our mission had been accomplished. I'll never know if Dr. Lilly placed the stoma on Carole LePage's markings, or if he found a different spot to make the opening. All I know is that I felt relieved and happy that I was really doing "everything by the book." I was supposed to have my ET nurse place those markings, and so we did. Actually, there was no great hurry. My parents and sisters were in the waiting room outside the surgery area and the hospital staff indicated to them, since they had just arrived, that they could see me for a few minutes in the OR holding room for patients waiting for surgery.

It was difficult to see my parents. Mothers and fathers the world over worry about their children, regardless of the age of their offspring. I could see the pain in my parents' eyes that they would not have wished for me to undergo any suffering. Ours is a close family and my parents and sisters would never have missed being with me on this special day. As Mom and Dad, Joanne, Margaret and Sister Joyce stood around my bed, I felt their loving presence.

We are also a praying family, so the most normal action was to reach out, hold each other's hands and recite together the Lord's Prayer, "Our Father...."

"Hail Mary, full of grace," my mother intoned as is her custom, being the mother of a large family. Many were the evenings we as family all gathered around the statue of the Blessed Virgin Mary in our living room and recited the rosary together for world peace. Now, we were praying for one of Mary's children, and I knew that I was held in the arms of my heavenly mother in a new way, being so entrusted by the members of my own dear family.

We all kissed each other and I was pushed away into the operating room. There is only a brief period of time before the anesthetics take effect and so I do not recall anything of the operation except closing my eyes and pretending that I was about to enter into a special journey within the recesses of my own body.

CHAPTER SIX

ON WINGS OF LOVE

I do recall upon waking up in intensive care that I was glad to be alive. There was not an unusual situation with my operation, but one is never one hundred percent certain that there will not be any complications or adverse reactions to anesthesia or that the body will sustain the trauma of the ordeal. I remember the first afternoon and evening and well into the night after surgery. I kept waking up and wanting to speak with everyone who was around. A blizzard and continuous snow storm kept my family from going home. Sister Mary Modesta and Sister Mary Renetta, the administrators of St. Mary Hospital, were kind to allow my parents and two of my sisters to remain in the hospital for the night, with accommodations in unused patients' rooms. Thus, throughout the night, usually every hour or two, one of them stopped in to see how I was doing. I recall having some conversations with each one of them--my parents and Joanne and Margaret about how much we meant to one another. It seems that when one's life is "on hold," there is time to step back and feel the emotions of love and gratitude that are so often hidden during the busy times of life--which is almost daily!

WALKING THROUGH THE WOODS

But I can still recall the strong feelings I had of just being alive and happy that everything went well.

The greatest pain was in the lower abdominal area because of the catheters for drainage, both for water elimination and from the rectal area. It was no fun to move with those tubes hanging out and each time I moved there was a most uncomfortable feeling.

Each member of the nursing staff was so patient and cheery, but I especially remember Carol, the nighttime nurse. She was my "life-line" to the outside world. Dr. Babu Paidipaty, the Director of the Critical Care Unit, was concerned that I not be disturbed by any visitors and had posted a "no visitors" sign--which meant no one was to visit except my immediate family. At first I resented this absolute ruling, but I came to guard and appreciate the quiet time just to recuperate without having to answer numerous phone calls and stay up to await visitors. So, my friends soon found out that when they called Carol, she would give a prompt update on my condition. She would let me know, "Your friends, Sister Colleen, Father Jim, and also Dr. Jean from Philadelphia all called today and said they're praying for you. Sister Nancy tried to see you, but I had to say 'Sorry, Doctor's orders!' You had many other friends stopping in today and I assured them all you were doing well. They all want to be remembered." And on and on.

One funny incident occured in the Critical Care unit when a dear friend, John Del Signore, sneaked in to see me by informing the staff that he was "my Italian brother." I don't know if anyone believed John, but I can imagine

34

when he walked in with a double breasted suit, top coat, and dark hat, that the staff figured they would not challenge this member of my family!

At last the day came when I was discharged from the critical care unit and assigned to a lovely room on the fifth floor. I was now allowed visitors. Sister Joyce, with her expert organizational skills, had already distributed the numerous floral arangements so that these could be given to the chapel and departments throughout the hospital for others to enjoy. Now, she was the "director of visitor traffic" as so many wonderful friends and family members wanted to come and visit. My University colleagues, Sister Mary Lauriana and Sister Rose Marie, were the first to bring wishes from our University family. Of course, I eagerly awaited the arrival of Sister Mary Dennis, the provincial superior of the Felician Sisters, to thank her for the concern, care and prayerful support of all of our sisters.

The very first night of visitors also brought Al and Doris Eichman and then John and Lina Del Signore, Carolyn and Don Di Como and Betty and Bill Phillips. All of these--and so many more that I cannot name them all-- formed a vital part of a support group with their loving prayers, concern, daily cards and get well wishes numbering in the hundreds. I can only hope that everyone who takes ill could have such a tremendous experience of being cared and carried on wings of love.

The word "wings" brings a special symbol into my mind. I remember little of the first day in the critical care unit, probably because of the pain medication. But there are angels hovering near who were part of that first day and all the days from that point onward.

The Holy Eucharist is for me as a Catholic and a religious sister an abiding source of strength and sustenance. Daily reception of the holy bread, the Body of Christ, is a special part of one's day. My daily "guardian angel" as I named Sister Mary Eucharita, would walk softly into the room at around 5:45 each morning bringing with her that Presence of the Lord which for me instilled healing and calm perhaps more potent than any pain medication.

The other symbol of angel wings hung above my bed. During one of the first evenings when I was hospitalized, the nurse on duty brought into the room a handmade angel which she said had been delivered by one of the students from Madonna University. Kathy Rodgers and her husband, Bill, had stopped by out of concern. I had not yet met them but her loving gift was indeed a symbol of the prayerful wishes I had received from countless students and faculty of the University. To this day the little angel with its white flowing robe and soft smiling face hangs as a guard above my bed. When my eyes light upon it I am reminded of the Creator who made heaven and earth and all angels and men and women who are messengers and harbingers of love.

Before I complete the reminiscing of my hospital stay I need to comment on the wonderful spirit and caring attitude I experienced from the medical and nursing staff, the various technicians and service personnel of St. Mary Hospital as they went about their daily tasks. They too, were ministering angels to me. Each morning I looked forward to seeing Linda as she cleaned up the room and shared a few moments about her family in between the strokes of the mop. And then there were the respiratory therapists and lab technicians who were all highly capable and personally thoughtful as they handled their daily routine duties. I appreciated each one of the nursing staff and aides of the fifth floor including Ursula, Sylvia, Annie, and Mary. I was grateful for the daily visits of my surgeon, Dr. Lilly, plus all of the "drop in" chats with Dr. Tactac, Dr. Joseph and Dr. Babu. Each one did all he could to answer any questions and, more importantly, to be present for a few moments of friendly exchange. I never felt as if I were treated as a patient--but rather a friend and colleague who was a welcomed partner in the healing process of my own body.

Madonna University Library and Kresge Hall Entrance, 1993.

CHAPTER SEVEN

FRANKIE JOINS THE FAMILY

One of the first persons to visit me following the surgery was Enzo Paparelli, a long standing friend of the University and of our family. Having sustained a similar operation some thirteen years earlier, and living with his delightful motto, "Have bag, will travel," Enzo, a fellow "ostomate," (the description of a person who has a stoma), came to assure me of a return to health and of some practical matters pertaining to the wearing of an appliance.

I felt close to him because of the shared experience and I didn't hesitate to inquire if he had named his stoma. No one actually suggested that I do, but a week after surgery when I began thinking of the finality of my decision and of the probable reality that I would use the stoma for elimination purposes for the remainder of my life, I decided to love that part of me in a tender way. I began to refer to my stoma as "Frankie." This is a special name. Each year I name the first monarch butterfly of the season, "Frankie," and my own name is a derivative from the name of the special lover of God, persons and all creatures--Saint Francis of Assisi, my patron saint. So, in January of 1992, "Frankie" became part of my life.

I said to Enzo, "Well, did you name your stoma?"

"Of course," he laughed, "she's Suzie."

I came to find out in speaking with other ostomates that our little friends have such names as "Igor," "Bobbie," Stash," and "Buttons." (Freud would have a field day discovering that most of the male ostomates name their stomas with female counterparts while we women choose masculine derivatives!)

The most important message I discovered is that loving is an important part of healing--the loving given by the Creator and Healer and the loving extended by ourselves and others in our human encounters.

Frankie soon made a great impression but it wasn't long before his middle name spelled "t-r-o-u-b-l-e"!

As a new ostomate I wanted to do everything just perfectly and tried to follow the detailed directions of my enterostomal therapist: "Always take an extra change of pouch when you come to the hospital for examinations." Five weeks after the colostomy operation I was scheduled for a CT scan. Well, about three minutes before I was to enter the testing room, I thought it best to go to the rest room and empty Frankie's pouch so I'd look my "best" for the pelvic pictures.

Everything went just fine until I flushed the toilet. In my left hand, reaching over for the handle, I held my pouch clamp. Suddenly I spied a lucky penny on the floor. Bending over I scooped it up with my right hand while flushing the toilet with my left. Yes, it happened. The clamp slipped out of hand and into the flowing waters of the bowl. I was left holding a shiny penny--not exactly the object one can use to secure the bottom of a colostomy pouch! Frankie began to panic. No problem. I had remembered to bring an extra change as previously instructed. But, where was the extra clamp? Not there! I had forgotten it. No rubber band, no hair pin, no paper clip; I had nothing to secure the pouch. The CT technician was knocking at the door that I was the next person for the test.

Rescue was near. I was in St. Mary Hospital and within one minute my enterostomal therapist, Carole LePage, brought a new clamp and I was once again ready to face the world. Lesson learned.

It is now my standard procedure to carry an extra pouch clamp closure in my pocket, next to that lucky penny.

Sister Mary Francilene and Sister Joyce Marie attending the Beatification Ceremony in Rome of Blessed Mary Angela Truszkowska, Foundress of the Felician Sisters, 1993.

CHAPTER EIGHT

MALIGNANT OR NOT,
THAT IS THE QUESTION

After the tenth person looked up, I began asking myself, "Why do people look at my hair when I mention that I am undergoing chemotherapy treatment?" It appears that it is an automatic reaction. Indeed, one of the many side effects of some types of chemotherapy is the temporary loss of hair during treatment. Not all patients, however, experience the same effects. Actually, cancer is a group of diseases. There are more than 100 different kinds of cancer, all of which attack cells of the human body. Something triggers cells to lose the ability to limit and direct their growth. Such cells divide too rapidly and grow without normal order. The malignant tumors formed by such growth can invade and destroy tissues and organs located near the original site of a cancer. Cancer cells can also enter the blood stream or the lymph system and spread or metastasize to other parts of one's body.

If I sound pedantic, it's because I read everything I

could put my hands on regarding cancer. When I was first diagnosed, I decided to handle this experience as I have most others in my life, by prayer and study. I told God, "You are my destiny, so if this is part of the challenge of my life, it's ultimately your body. But I will use every part of my brain, heart, mind and spirit, not to fight the disease, but rather to cooperate with the defenses You have given me, and those of medical science, to effect a retreat of the enemy!"

Among my studies, I reviewed the stages of cancer. This was important to me in order to review with the medical staff the appropriate treatment of my disease. Some 40 years ago, the Dukes system divided cancer into several stages. These have been modified through the years. More recently, the American Joint Committee on Cancer (AJCC) developed a staging system that takes into account some important factors that influence the prognosis of specific cases.

In either staging system, my tumor appeared to be Stage B2 according to the modified Dukes system or Stage II if I referenced the TNM system developed by the AJCC. (TNM represents T = tumor size; N = any lymph node involvement; M = the degree if any of metastasis.)

The description of my tumor was that it had penetrated the bowel wall and some cancer cells were discovered in the fatty tissue surrounding the bowel, but there was no evidence of cancer invasion of adjacent organs or lymph nodes. All 17 of the pericolonic lymph nodes which had been removed during surgery proved negative for any metastatic tumor.

Research now told me, as did my team of doctors, that adjuvant therapy treatment was the next step in the journey toward a positive prognosis. (I always use the word 'cure,' although the doctors do not use this word--at least not yet.)

But in reaching out for such a reality, I found myself setting forth with renewed enthusiasm and positive attitude so as to be counted among the survivors of cancer.

I spent one Sunday afternoon studying up on the survival rates of colorectal cancer. I've found over a period of time that the initial feeling of "this is somebody else," gradually turned to the realization that "this is me in one of these stages and one of these categories. I want to hope for the cure."

Again, the survival rates, I read, correlated with the stages of cancer. Pouring through the 1992 edition of the "Textbook of Medicine," in the University library I found my research. The 10-year survival rate is 50% for patients with colorectal cancer after surgical resection and standard therapy of 5-fluorouracil (5-FU) and radiation therapy. Those odds didn't set too well. Again, I've never pulled back my prayer to the Lord that He's in control and I'll live as long as His plans call for it, but I still have that natural longing of every human being to live a long, healthy and productive life over a normal lifespan.

Back to the stats. The survival rates increase with each lowered stage. (That's the positive way I want to describe these data because it sounds so foreboding to state that with each progressive stage, the survival rate decreases.) Anyway, for Stage II, the present survival rate is 70-80% with the prescribed adjuvant therapies. Now, that sounded more like it. Bring on the radiation! Where do I get those shots of 5-FU? Hurry up, I want to live!

My therapy consisted of three treatments in one week of 5-FU chemotherapy, followed by six weeks of daily rounds of radiation consisting of 180 Rad per day for a total of 5040 Rad, with a final series of 12 weeks of weekly chemotherapy.

Dr. Dan Benvenisti is the oncologist treating me, having his medical specialty in hematology and oncology. I had met him some five years previous to my encounter with cancer when we both served on the board of directors of Angela Hospice. At times we sat across from one another during the evening meetings. I never thought I'd be the one to need his medical services as we discussed during the meeting times the role of medication and patient needs of the hospice clients.

About one week following my surgery "Dr. Ben," as he is known on the staff of St. Mary Hospital, dropped into my hospital room. He introduced himself again and indicated that Dr. Lilly had referred me to him and to Dr. Omar Majid, a radiation oncologist, as the team to commence the adjuvant therapies as soon as the perineal wound would be sufficiently healed.

Actually, I was glad at that point that I had searched the research files and the medical books prior to my own surgery. I felt more knowledgeable and ready to ask the medical team questions. For me, this was a critical point. I wanted to be an active member of my own medical team, not a silent and inactive bystander upon whom the medical profession would look upon as a statistic. I have much gratitude and respect for all those of the medical staff who provided this scenario for me. Each doctor, nurse and technician was willing to answer my many questions and entered into the discussion of my case with enthusiasm and insight.

Now, back to Dr. Ben. I began the series of chemotherapy 5-FU intravenous shots in his office. From the beginning, it was never any trouble driving to the hospital because of the close proximity to the University. For this, I was fortunate. The appointments were set either early in the morning before the working day, or at lunch time. Basically, I was able to function in my responsibilities by balancing work time with some rest when needed. I found that by mid-afternoon on "chemo" days I became increasingly fatigued. Upon occasion there was also some nausea, but this was never to any great extent. Fatigue and skin rashes were the most prevalent reactions I experienced with the chemotherapy.

One evening I remember using the elevator from the ground to the third floor where my bedroom is located. I was so tired that I sat on the floor of the elevator in the corner and felt that I never wanted to move again. I just sat there and went up and down for a few minutes until I said, "This is silly. Pull yourself together and go rest!" I did that on more than one occasion. In fact, for most days in the first three months after surgery, I required more rest periods in between the working hours. But, that too, passed with each succeeding week.

"Sunny" is a most appropriate name for the helpful receptionist who first greeted me on the day I was

introduced to the radiation therapy staff. Together with
Sherri, her associate (i.e., the "Sunny and Cher" team!), I
was always made to feel welcome as I stepped into the
department which would become a part of my daily
routine.

The most unfamiliar territory, however, was the
radiation room itself.   The first time I went in for
measurements and a simulation session, I fought off a
series of fears. First, I was concerned that the doctor who
did the markings on the x-ray charts was not the one with
whom I was familiar through all the past visits and
discussions. Dr. Omar Majid had left for a trip to India
and Dr. James Gamero was the physician handling the
patients for a two- to three-week period.   He has a
respected reputation and I'm certain that I had trust in his
ability and yet, I thought, What if he radiates the stoma
area? Did Dr. Majid discuss my case with him before he
left for India?   Does this doctor know that I want to
understand everything about my case and I don't want to be
a silent patient? And so it went. I recognize that my
irrationality was borne of fear and not based in reality.
But, for me, these thoughts were real. Just as real was my
concern that the technicians might mix up the lead-alloy
shaping blocks which were to be placed in the machine to
block the radiation from effecting the non-cancerous
portion of the abdominal area, with those of my father who
had been treated for prostate cancer by the radiation staff.

Now I can laugh at myself and even share these silly
musings. But, at the time, I held these fears inside and
took a careful look at the machine and the name on the

blocks and made sure at least for myself that everything was in order. In thinking back on the radiation weeks, it would have been better if I had shared my unfounded concerns with John Schwartz, the Department Head or Patricia Aho, the nurse, or with one of the technicians such as George, Kathy or Rekha, so as to alleviate some of the concern. But, as in other areas of my life, so here also, I wanted to appear calm and undisturbed. However, in speaking with other patients in similar situations, I have found that they likewise, have experienced at least some type of trepidation when facing a new medical challenge.

These thoughts didn't last too long. I decided to "make friends" with the radiation machinery. The prescription called for approximately six weeks of daily radiation treatments. From the first day of treatment, I used a visualization technique and pretended I was relaxing on a beach in Florida. "Well, here I am for another tanning session," I'd whisper to "Big-X," the name I gave the machine. Once the door closed and I was alone on my stomach for the ten to fifteen-minute time period, I'd imagine a beautiful sky with the soft sand beneath me. That was a particularly good scene because the hard, narrow treatment table was anything but soft.

On some days, especially when I felt moved in a more spiritual vein, I'd imagine that I was enjoying the company of the Lord and would say to Him, "Well, Lord, I'm here getting warmed by Your Love. Burn out of me not only the cancer, but also all that is hard within me--all that needs purification, especially my pride and lack of charity."

WALKING THROUGH THE WOODS

Those moments of prayer were among my best during the long weeks of treatment and I soon experienced a greater sense of peace and calm within my body and spirit.

As I recalled earlier, the greatest reactions I had from the therapies were fatigue and RASHES! I would go from one rash to the next. It seemed as if I were allergic to either the plastic of the appliance or the tape used to secure it. Aveeno baths, cortisone creams, assorted salves, medicated powders--nothing gave much relief. It was probably a matter of time and the body's need to become more tolerant of all the treatments I was undergoing. Approximately five months after the treatments had ceased, there was much less irritability of the skin. The best solution I found during the time of the rashes was baby oil. I found that when the skin was more moist and less dry, the tendency to scratch and make the situation worse, was decreased.

All in all, I am grateful to the physicians and the medical personnel who assisted me during the weeks and months of therapy. It was worth the inconveniences, reactions and minor irritants when one thinks of the alternative. My body and spirit have risen to new heights. My health appears better now than it had been for many months in the past. Is there yet any malignancy? I do not know. The periodic blood tests and CT scans continue. Can I say that I am less fearful than in the past? I would say, "Yes!" Have I learned to trust more? I'm certainly trying to enter more deeply into the next phase of my life with its wondering and waiting moments while living my life to its fullest.

CHAPTER NINE

WALKING THROUGH THE WOODS

The woods are lovely, dark and deep.
But I have promises to keep,
And miles to go before I sleep,
And miles to go before I sleep.

> "Stopping by Woods on a Snowy Evening"
> *Collected Poems* of Robert Frost
> Garden City, New York, 1942

I don't remember the first time I read the poems of Robert Frost, but often throughout my life I recall the haunting image of the woods and its call to my inner soul. Among my favorite activities for "free time"--which doesn't happen too often--is finding wherever there are woods and paths or non-paths.   Within the silence and coolness of the tree culture I have often found the answers to my questions, the healing of hurts, and the understanding of quieting the mind, heart and soul. Sometimes I go with a friend, but most often I go alone.

WALKING THROUGH THE WOODS

I read, I hum a tune, I walk and listen, and I pray. I had missed the woods during the months of surgery, treatments and convalescence. Truly I found consolation in visits to the chapel, in the quiet of my own room, among family and friends, but I waited for the day I could return to the woods.

That day arrived on April 18, "Holy Saturday" morning, the day before Easter 1992. In the soft early morning hours I walked through the Kensington Park woods with an excitement I can rekindle today. The day marked a little over three months from the date of cancer surgery and I was alive and breathing deeply of fresh pine needles and listening to the morning melodies of the winged birds. I walked slowly. There was no doubt that my stamina was not fully there with me. It was difficult climbing up "Fox Trail," but I made it because that's where most of the deer "hang out" although I never quite figured out why they never correctly read the signs for "Deer Run" because these graceful inhabitants tended to stay on "Fox Trail" and also on "Chickadee Loop"!

There was, however, something different about my emotions on this day. Indeed, I felt a personal satisfaction in having the energy to undertake a decidedly long hike. But, there was a more deep-seated reason for coming alone that day. I had to forgive myself. A few of my friends had asked discreetly if I had experienced any anger, despondency or discouragement over the events of the past few months. Thinking back, I can honestly say such moments and days were few. I tended to accept the experience as a challenge. I was never angry with God, nor did I ask, "Why me, Lord?" If there was any anger to be resolved it was with myself.

No doctor, no family member or friend ever criticized me for the length of time I actually had symptoms before I went to see a physician. But I knew the truth. For about two years I had experienced unpleasant digestive gas, mild diarrhea and some blood in the stool. Because these symptoms seemed to disappear, I watched my diet and thought it was a case of irritated bowel. The final four months, however, I began to suspect something was not right when the stool became very stringy and the blood was present with each elimination. I never did have any pain. But my exaggerated fear of physical examinations led me to hold off making any appointments, again thinking that the symptoms were not permanent. Finally, I felt an emerging "glob" each time I eliminated which then retracted into the rectum. I now know that this was a large polyp described as a villous adenoma and that although it in itself was not malignant, a subsequent biopsy indicated a tumor in the bowel wall from which this large polyp had grown.

During the months of diagnosis, surgery, radiation, chemotherapy and recuperation I had put the thought of my own responsibility in the back recesses of my mind. I did not want to acknowledge that if I had gone to a doctor sooner perhaps the tumor would not have grown to the extent that it did. The reason I choose to be so graphic in the description of my symptoms is to encourage my family members and friends who read my thoughts to take the positive steps toward examinations which can be preventive

WALKING THROUGH THE WOODS

in nature to the onset of a serious illness. In any case, whenever I entered the woods as a setting for prayer, the same as in my room, or in the chapel, I needed to face the core of my anger. Even with years of intelligent decision making and education, I failed to interpret the signs of my own body and respond to these with immediate attention rather than fear and hesitation.

So on April 18, 1992, I confronted my anger in the middle of the woods. I cried because of the uncertainty of the prognosis. Time was on my side because the tumor had not been metastatic in its progression, and the statistics were becoming more and more successful for persons undergoing radiation and chemotherapy for colorectal cancer with subsequent non-recurrence.

But I felt stupid, humiliated, frustrated and angry with myself for waiting so long before attending to the existing symptoms.

Within two hours, however, I experienced a great calm and peace once I had asked God for forgiveness and myself for the months of unnecessary pain and struggle. I even smiled because I recalled how St. Francis of Assisi, my holy patron, had asked the Lord to forgive his body, "Brother Ass," as he called himself for abusing his body during life and not always caring for it.

I truly laughed out loud to the surprise of two deer standing in the woods because the "Brother Ass" part was so appropriate in my case! So I dared to say, "Lord, forgive me, Sister Ass, for losing that part of my body to cancer, but I will not lose my heart nor my soul in the process...."

Walking Through the Woods

Since that day in the woods I KNOW that there is no cancer in my spirit and I am at great peace with the reconciliation that has happened within me. There is no more blame. There is no anger. There is no questioning, "What if?" I am a blessed person. I am held in the hand of the Lord. I know His presence in my life, within my body and spirit. I awake at night and thank God for the tremendous experience of this "pre-death" gift. I am no longer afraid of pain nor of death. I cannot say much more than this except that in coming to grips with the anger I had within me, the replacement of this emotion with serenity is often more than I can describe.

I have chosen to title my reflections *Walking Through the Woods,* because it was through the darkness of the shadows of the trees, through the deep silence of the branches and through the encounter with their Creator that I was given the courage, insight and joy to walk the remainder of my life in the Light.

Kensington Metro Park, 1994.

CHAPTER TEN

THE GOD OF DETAILS AND SURPRISES

The famous concert of July 7, 1990 of "the three tenors," namely José Carreras, Placido Domingo and Luciano Pavarotti, under the baton of maestro Zubin Mehta, enjoyed eighteen months as the most favored music compact disc and video produced that year. For me, however, the enthralling music as performed at the Baths of Caracalla in Rome, became a soothing balm and an integral experience of my own healing process.

I would listen many times over and view the video while adopting as my personal theme song the haunting melody and words of "Nessun Dorma" from Puccini's *Turandot*.

...Depart, oh night! Set, you stars!
Set, you stars! At dawn I shall win!
I shall win! I shall win!

After reading the autobiography of José Carreras, *Singing of the Soul* (1989), which detailed the discovery, diagnosis and subsequent hospitalization in 1987 and treatment for acute lymphoblastic leukemia, I felt a soul relationship with him. I looked forward to somehow meeting him in person, if only to thank him for the inspiration of his writing and life experience in my own struggle with cancer.

The opportunity came. The Detroit newspapers announced that José Carreras would be performing May 26, 1992 at the Fisher Theater for a one-night concert as part of an American concert tour to raise funds for the José Carreras International Leukemia Foundation. This was the opportunity for which I had hoped! However, to see Mr. Carreras in a private afterglow immediately following the concert, the ticket price was $375. This was definitely out of the reach of a nun's monthly stipend! What to do?

There were balcony seats available for $25 and I was able to receive as a gift two such tickets to attend the concert. It didn't matter that the seats were in row "R" of the very top balcony! Just to attend the concert was a great treat. Sister Mary Giovanni Monge and I went to the event. It was a special moment for both of us since Sister "Gio" not only appreciates opera but she was a personal "angel of mercy" for me in days immediately following my surgery. She had generously offered her time to assist in the cleansing of the perineal wound and to "line up" Frankie's pouch until I became familiar with all the details of the change process.

In any case, May 26, was a banner day. The date signaled the final radiation treatment after a six-week daily program of pelvic radiation. And, now we were on our way to attend the José Carreras concert!

The God of Details and Surprises

So many times in my life I have found that even my innermost wishes have been answered. Today I secretly wished to have the opportunity to see and speak with José. In my own prayer moments the Lord has often whispered, "Your wish is my command," although it should be the other way around. Nevertheless, whatever I dare to wish or pray for so often happens that I praise and thank the God of details and surprises! Such was the experience we would have during the evening of May 26, 1992.

The first half of the concert was superb with José reaching the high notes with his warm and lustrous voice, rendering perfect diction and intense expression. The theater was overflowing. Due to a computer error, some of the seats had been sold twice. Before the concert had begun, persons were searching for any possible empty seats. More than one hundred chairs had been placed on the stage behind the singer to accommodate the sold out crowd. No one minded the inconvenience. All knew that tonight would be another memorable experience with José Carreras. Here was one of the world's greatest tenors who had survived a life-threatening year and had returned in good health to share his talents with renewed vigor and commitment.

At the intermission I said to Sister Giovanni, "Let's go down to the main floor and inquire if there are any empty seats closer to the stage."

Now, this would seem to be an impossibility given the pressure to locate seats for the overflowing crowd, but, my thought was an attempt to move closer to the stage so we could make a "dive" to get backstage once the concert was over.

Why should I be surprised by what we found!   In answer to our query regarding empty seats, one of the ushers responded that there were indeed two seats at the end of row "R" on the main floor which had not been occupied during the first part of the concert!

For the remainder of the concert, there we were--two excited nuns perched at the edge of two seats down in the main right section--and for all we knew, these could be the $375 seats!

The experience was breathtaking. We could see the singer's expressions, the intensity of his entire body as he rendered the music of Massenet, Puccini, Verdi and Guastavino.   When the final strains of the encore, "Granada," concluded, we both attempted as spawning fish to "swim" upwards toward the front of the stage as the entire audience was moving to the rear exits. We made it to the front steps of stage left but were promptly instructed that we would need the permission of the stage manager who presently was at stage right. Hurriedly we went to the rear of stage right. Five or six persons were there waiting to have their copies of José's autobiography autographed by the singer.   We were instructed that it was, however, highly unlikely that we would be able to meet with Mr. Carreras because he was scheduled to attend a reception.

Undaunted, the small group proceeded backstage and waited. And waited. And waited. Finally, a gentleman who appeared to be a coordinator of the event came down the stairs from the second floor where Mr. Carreras was in the dressing room. He stated that we most probably would not see the singer because he was not scheduled to come down this way and there was no certainty how long he would remain at the reception being held in another section of the building.

I walked up to the man and handed him a small bag inquiring if he would be so kind and see that Mr. Carreras would receive this gift. It contained two T-shirts for his children, Alberto, 18, and Julia, 13 years of age. Knowing that teenagers live in T-shirts for the most part, I was certain they would enjoy this gift from the bookstore of Madonna University. The man graciously said he would deliver the gift.

Should we wait longer? I asked Sister Gio about her time knowing that she needed to wake up early the next morning to attend 6:10 a.m. Mass and to conduct her duties as director of Angela Hospice. No problem. We would stay until 11:00 p.m. just to see if Mr. Carreras would appear. It was now 10:40 p.m.

Five minutes later Sister Gio poked me and said, "There is your bag!" A gentleman had descended from the second floor elevator and was carrying a tuxedo on a hanger; around the top of the hanger was the bag I had sent upstairs. I followed the man out to the car only to learn that he was "Richard," the limousine driver for José Carreras and pianist, Lorenzo Bavaj.

Richard confirmed two points: first, he was the favored driver of the travel agency who booked him for visiting dignitaries and, secondly, he would be meeting the two gentlemen at this very door probably in about fifteen minutes. We waited.

WALKING THROUGH THE WOODS

True to expectations, we soon heard the lilting voice of José Carreras as he arrived back stage thanking his hosts. When I first saw him I felt an emotional jolt. Here was a "fellow sufferer" who had endured much more pain than I ever did; who had exposed his soul in his autobiography and who had not hesitated to share his past struggles and the present resurrection he knew after his return to health. The tears came to my eyes when I thought of this special moment of meeting. As he approached us, I handed him my name card and said, "Thank you, José, for tonight's magnificent concert, and especially for your life." As I indicated the copy of his autobiography which Sister Giovanni was holding, I looked directly into his eyes and said, "Please pray for me, I'm a fellow patient." In one second he grasped the intent of my words and then reached over with a big hug and smile, "If you pray for me, too!"

He was delighted to know of the two T-shirts for his children because we told him he had no time for shopping with his busy concert schedule! José autographed our copy of his book and then he was gone with Richard the trusted driver.

I don't know if and when we shall meet again. I only know that the details and surprises of May 26, 1992 bring a warm smile to my face when I remember a good and loving God who arranges such encounters.

THE FINAL CHAPTER

...Christ will be exalted through me, whether I live or die. For, to me, 'life' means Christ; hence dying is so much gain. If, on the other hand, I am to go on living in the flesh, that means productive toil for me--and I do not know which I prefer. I am strongly attracted to both: I long to be freed from this life and to be with Christ, for that is the far better thing; yet it is more urgent that I remain alive for your sakes...

Paul to the Philippians, 1:20-24
The New American Bible

This Scripture passage continues to invade me. I think I've come to understand its meaning each time I must go into the hospital for another series of CT scans, blood profile and examinations. The question looms, "What if more cancer cells are discovered?" Just when I feel that I have quite forgotten about myself and daily life has evolved into a nice routine of work, prayer, rest, and relaxation, an appointment time rolls around, or some newspaper article about the continued research studies on cancer rouse me from my complacency. I can feel the anxiety level rise and the need to know the test results as soon as possible--with a big smile and shout of excitement when the results are positive. BUT, there is the nagging concern about the rise in the CEA levels, modest though these are, and the subtle questioning about what ever happened to those cancer cells that "penetrated the bowel wall" from the very first surgery/biopsy report.

And so, I sway between the states of euphoria and depression while striving to keep hope and faith in the necessary proportions in my life. Yet I know that the "final chapter" is beyond me. In the silence of quiet prayer I begin to know the subsiding of anxiety and the increase of trust in the Lord. During those moments I begin to echo the words of St. Paul that life or death mean the same to me. I could accept either one with equal love. But when I am deep in the throes of busy ministerial activity I know the longing to be of service to my community and to the people in my life for many years to come.

I visit with our aging parents and I want to be with them especially during the last years of their life journey. It would not be normal for them to bury a daughter before their deaths. During the past year I've attended the funerals of five of my friends who have died from the effects of cancer and I am reminded of my own mortality. When the latest information comes in the mail from the National Cancer Institute, I read with growing interest the most recent statistics of persons living with and surviving colorectal cancer and I wonder if I will be one of those living in five years as a result of the modern advances made in detection and therapy for any recurrence of the disease.

The Final Chapter

As I write these words I think about what else I should or could ponder to include in this brief work. It must come to an end, yet I'm not certain how the epilogue would read. What I have written has come from my heart, soul and mind. My fears, hopes, joys and wonderings have surfaced during these past eighteen to twenty months more so than in the fifty-two years of my life to this date. In truth, I feel good about that.

I have wanted to share these thoughts with you who have chosen to spend a few moments reading my reflections. You may never have cancer. But without a doubt, sometime in life you will experience new waves of fear, pain, loss, hope and joy. The wonderful part of being alive, however, is that the moments of joy, happiness, strength and the abiding presence of the Lord outweigh the moments of struggle. The final chapter is Love.

"Guess Who's Playing the Classics?" Guest disc jockey for WQRS Radio Station, 1992.

66

EPILOGUE

When I had prepared the previous chapters for mailing to the publisher on June 27, 1994, little did I realize that within two weeks I would be writing this epilogue. On that exact date I was once again under the knife of a surgeon for the recurrence of cancer.

The previous month I had sought a second opinion regarding recent scans and tests which indicated cancer activity. Upon the recommendation of Thomas V. Angott, Chairman of the Board of the Michigan Cancer Foundation, himself a cancer patient and a dear friend, and with the full support of my medical team, I was examined by Dr. Vainutis K. Vaitkevicius, fondly known as, "Dr. V, the Cancer Doctor." As President of the Michigan Cancer Foundation and Professor of Medicine at Wayne State University, "Dr. V" is nationally recognized for his exceptional diagnostic talents.

Thus, Monday, June 27, 1994 found me at Harper Hospital, one of the twenty-eight comprehensive cancer centers in the United States, undergoing surgery for the removal of a large cystic mass which position in the pelvis also occasioned a total hysterectomy.

I offer my gratitude to Dr. Donald W. Weaver of University Surgeons and his team for preserving and extending my life through the wonders of modern technology, efficient surgery and above all, the presence of the Divine Physician whose healing presence is most evident in the remarkable resilience the human body has in sustaining pain and reacting to the healing process.

The reason I chose to write this epilogue before

EPILOGUE

Walking Through the Woods was actually published had to do more with new emotions experienced after surgery for recurrent cancer that were not necessarily part of the first experience. I remember one of my friends asking the year after the colostomy surgery whether I had bouts of depression and despair. I never did. There was always a great sense of hope as I described in previous chapters of this book. Another friend had said, "Don't you have any down days? You sound so upbeat and you write so optimistically. What do you do when you face the down days?"

The night that I left the hospital and returned to our convent infirmary which is a very quiet, beautiful and restful setting for recuperation, I did experience one of the most traumatic evenings and nights of my life. It is difficult to describe it, but it was a total feeling of desolation. It was not despair. It was, however, a feeling that my body had so dramatically changed that I was somewhat afraid of it. I felt that my inner organs had been ripped out. It was a feeling of having a part of life wrenched from within. My mother shared with me later that that is due to having a hysterectomy. I would agree, but it was more than that. It was a feeling of fear that although the cancer had been encapsulated in the pelvic area and had not spread to any other organs, could there still be cancer cells lurking in my body? Would I have the strength to put up a good fight as I had the first time and go through all the imaging, the visual techniques, the spiritual strengthening and the holistic approach to being totally healed?

EPILOGUE

I share this in the epilogue because that night was the most difficult and depressing time that I have ever experienced. I wanted to leave my room and go out in the middle of the field and just curl up and cry. Since I was too weak to leave the bed, I did have a good cry. But after the expression of these emotions, I knew what I had to do. The tapes, the records, the thoughts had to be changed. The rest of the night I spent listening to quiet music, playing over and over again the recording of *Chant* by the Benedictine Monks of Santo Domingo de Silos and, of course, my favorite *Three Tenors in Concert: Carreras, Domingo and Pavarotti*. Late at night I was once again transported to the famous Baths of Caracalla in Rome on a brilliant starlit night of July 7, 1990. I also recommitted my spirit, my emotions, my body and my will to the Divine Creator. I asked for returning peace to invade my soul and to remove the depths of depression. The morning dawn brought relief and the return of my resolve to continue my life in trust and serenity. I am more determined than ever to develop a healthy attitude of living with cancer, not dying from it...at least, not yet!

Additional chemotherapy will follow with a good prognosis for return to health. I look forward to the nineteenth year in serving as President of Madonna University. I also have two immediate goals. The first is to make a dentist appointment to replace an old filling with a good lifetime crown. Secondly, in three weeks I'll be at Kensington Metro Park to walk through the woods. This time there will be no anger, only deep gratitude that there are more hills to climb and many more days to live and love.